LOVE IS HELL

A CARTOON BOOK BY MATT GROENING

SPIFFY NEW INTRODUCTION JUST AHEAD

DESPITE ITS TITLE, THIS BOOK IS FOR DEBORAH

LYNDA BARRY IS STILL FUNK QUEEN OF THE GALAXY

FOR INFO, WRITE: THE LIFE IN HELL CARTOON CO., P.O. BOX 2879, VENICE, CA 90294 USA

Library of Congress Cataloging-in-Publication Data

Groening, Matt.
Love is hell.

Selections from the author's comic strip Life in hell.
I. Title. II: Title: Life in hell.
PN6728.L49G7 1986 741.5'973 85-43459
ISBN 0-679-75665-5

Printed in Mexico

6 8 9 7

Introduction

Yikes, ten years. It's been ten long years since *Love Is Hell* was published. I look back on these decade-old cartoons with the wisdom and weariness of a grizzled, veteran cartoonist, and I think:

Man, what a scam.

I didn't know anything about love back then. I was completely screwed up on the subject. I'd had a few relationships here and there, but for some reason they kept blowing up in my face. I couldn't figure it out.

I don't think it was my personality, which was fetching enough. I was even willing to fetch on occasion, if the girlfriend demanded it. But that wasn't enough. It may have been external reality, now that I think about it.

I had no money. I barely scraped together my rent every month by cartooning, writing ad copy for third-rate horror movies, and thinking up vaguely suggestive greeting cards. This was not as glamorous as it sounds. I drove a 1962 Dodge Dart, which had the unfortunate tendency to shake violently between 35 and 45 mph, and this made for plenty of frightened first and last dates. I lived in a sleazy Hollywood apartment in a neighborhood buzzed nightly by police helicopters, with lots of random gunfire to lull you to sleep, and this caused some of the less adventurous women in my life to refuse to visit my part of town after dark.

A few women did agree to go out with me anyway, but they didn't last too long. Sooner or later I'd show up at their apartments, ready for another cheap night out, and they'd say the meanest, most vicious things you can say to another person. Things like:

"We have to talk."

And:

"This just isn't working out."

And the most horrible of all:

"I hope we can still be friends."

So I'd slink back to my dinky, messy bachelor pad, sit at the wobbly card table in my kitchen, and draw another installment of "Life in Hell." The comic strip was my ongoing therapy, and I must now confess that *Love Is Hell* is a self-help book, with me being the self that was barely being helped.

What I found out when I started publishing cartoons about love is that there are tons of people so desperate for any clue about their miserable love lives that they will even check out cartoons with bulgy-eyed rabbits pontificating on the subject. Did I have any special love knowledge? Nope. Do I know the Secret of Love? Ha! Are there really "Nine Types of Girlfriends"? Beats me. But I did have nine panels to fill that week.

There is a happy ending to all this. I started dating this one particular woman, Deborah Caplan, who tolerated both my shaky Dodge Dart and my crummy apartment. On November 1, 1984, she offered to publish *Love Is Hell* herself. I said OK, and a month later, unbelievably enough, Deborah had the book out.

Love Is Hell sold well, the Dodge Dart bit the dust, I moved to a nicer but still dangerous neighborhood, Deborah and I got married, a decade passed, and I started writing this tenth-anniversary *Love Is Hell* introduction. During this time I drew a long series of comic strips about relationships featuring Akbar and Jeff, several of which are included in this book. The reason why I draw a strip with Akbar and Jeff instead of Binky and Sheba is that I figure no one can accuse me of trying to score points against men or women if the characters are identical.

But Deborah sees through that. She reads my comic strip every week, then says, "You think you're Jeff, and you think I'm Akbar, but someday the world will know the truth. You're really Akbar."

I must admit, she may be right. But which one is Akbar?

Matt Groening
Los Angeles
July 1994

AND NOW, LADIES AND GENTLEMEN, THIS COMIC STRIP TAKES GREAT PLEASURE IN PRESENTING

A 13-CHAPTER MINISERIES
BROUGHT TO YOU IN TEENY WEENY EYESTRAIN-O-VISION

THE SLANG OF LOVE

DESPITE MEDIA REPORTS TO THE CONTRARY, ASTUTE LUVOLOGISTS (SCIENTISTS OF LOVE) HAVE POINTED OUT THAT LOVE IS NO COUNTRY HAYRIDE. AS EVIDENCE, THEY OFFER THOUSANDS OF UNDERGROUND STREET TERMS FOR "LOVE." HERE ARE BUT A FEW:

LOOPY
JELLYBONES
THE TREMORS
MUSH-BRAIN
WHIRLORAMA
PALPITATIONS
SLIP 'N' SLIDE
BRICK-IN-THE-FACE
SLOP 'N' MOP
THE GOOEYS
BUCKET-O-CLAMS

WHAT THE GREAT PHILOSOPHERS HAVE SAID VIS-À-VIS LOVE

"LOVE IS A SLIPPERY EEL THAT BITES LIKE HELL." -- BERTRAND RUSSELL

"LOVE IS A PERKY ELF DANCING A MERRY LITTLE JIG AND THEN SUDDENLY HE TURNS ON YOU WITH A MINIATURE MACHINE-GUN." -- KIERKEGAARD

"LOVE IS A SNOWMOBILE RACING ACROSS THE TUNDRA AND THEN SUDDENLY IT FLIPS OVER, PINNING YOU UNDERNEATH. AT NIGHT, THE ICE WEASELS COME." --NIETZSCHE

CHAPTER I:
WHAT IS LOVE?

AND WHAT MAKES YOU THINK YOU DESERVE SOME?

FIG. 1
TYPICAL LOVE MANUEVER

WHOOPS.

FIG. 2

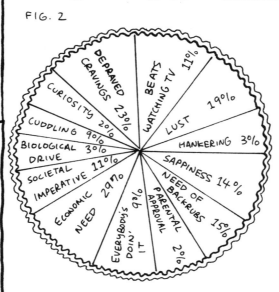

THE LOVE PIE

LOVE STOPPER'S TEXTBOOK

WATCH OUT FOR THESE EARLY WARNING SIGNS OF LOVE:
BOUNCY STEP
GOO-GOO EYES
BABBLING
BORED FRIENDS

LA LA LA

THE 9-HEADED HYDRA OF LOVE

FIG. 3

LOVE, LOVE ME DO

CRUSH
INFATUATION
SEDUCTION
NARCISSISM
OBSESSION
UNFOCUSED HORNINESS
DESIRE
INSANITY
FOCUSED HORNINESS
TRUE LOVE

WHY YOU MIGHT FEEL UNLOVED:

☐ YOU ARE SUCH A DREADFUL PERSON THAT NO ONE COULD POSSIBLY LOVE YOU.

☐ YOU ARE THE ONLY ONE WHO REALLY EXISTS IN THE UNIVERSE, AND THE REST OF US ARE JUST PHANTOM IMAGES.

☐ WHO THE HELL CARES?

THE SECRET OF LOVE

A SPECIAL NOTE FOR ADVANCED LOVE EXPERTS ONLY:

THE SECRET OF LOVE IS -- WAIT A MINUTE. SOMEONE WHO SHOULD KNOW BETTER IS PEEKING. SO YOU THINK YOU'RE AN ADVANCED LOVE EXPERT, EH? YOU OUGHTA BE ASHAMED.

NEXT: LOVE VS. FREEDOM

©1984 BY MATT GROENING

A SPECIAL 13-CHAPTER BONUS FUN SERIES! COLLECT 'EM ALL! YOU FORGOT LAST WEEK'S IN WHICH YOU TO CLIP STRIP, CASE (NOT FOR FORGET IT. RESPONSIBLE ADVICE TAKEN.)

LOVE IS HELL

CHAPTER II:
THE 57 VARIETIES OF LOVE

LOVE MONGER'S TEXTBOOK

AVOID SHARING AFFECTION WITH PEOPLE WEARING DESPERATE T-SHIRTS.

WILL YOU BE MY FRIEND?

IN WESTERN TRADITION, THERE HAVE BEEN APPROXIMATELY FOUR KINDS, OR FLAVORS, OF LOVE. THESE INCLUDE:

① "PHILIA" FRIENDSHIP, BROTHERLY LOVE — HEY PAL. YO.

② "EROS" THE DRIVE TO CREATE OR PROCREATE — VOILA

③ "AGAPE" THE LOVE WHICH IS DEVOTED TO THE OTHER — TRY THESE YUMMY APPETIZERS. OK

④ "LUST" THE CURRENT FAVORITE — HI PAL. YO.

BUT IN THESE COMPLEX MODERN FINAL DAYS, THE WHOLE CONCEPT OF LOVE HAS EXPLODED LIKE A CORNUCOPIA WITH A STICK OF DYNAMITE STUCK IN IT. THE MESS IS EVERYWHERE. IN FACT, YOU PROBABLY GOT SOME FLICKED ON YOU RIGHT NOW AND YOU DON'T EVEN KNOW IT.

SCIENTISTS WORKING LATE INTO THE NIGHT HAVE NOW ISOLATED SOME 57 VARIETIES OF LOVE. WHAT IS PECULIAR, THEY NOTE, IS THAT MANY OF THESE LOVE-VARIETIES INTERACT SIMULTANEOUSLY, CAUSING MUCH JOY, ECSTASY, CONFUSION, AND FUCK-UPS.

THIS IS CALLED THE "LOVE BLENDER EFFECT";

HENCE THE POPULAR STREET CRY:

I'VE JUST BEEN THROUGH THE LOVE BLENDER!!!

I CAN DIG IT.

WILL YOU BE MY FRIEND.

THE LOVE BLENDER®

DON'T TOUCH THAT DIAL

FRAPPE · SHRED · PUREE · WHIRL · REND ASUNDER · LIQUEFY

THE 57 VARIETIES OF LOVE

INFATUATION   CRUSH   STUPEFACTION
PUPPY LOVE   FLAME   CALF LOVE   WHEE
PLATONIC LOVE   ARDOR   YEN
PERFECT LOVE   WEIRD YEARNING   SELF-LOVE   WOO
ANIMAL MAGNETISM   VEGETABLE MAGNETISM
ITCHY LOVE   OBSESSION   PURE LOVE   YA-YA-YA
WHAT-THE-HELL LOVE   STRONG LIKE
BEE-YOOP   SLOPPY LOVE   THROBBING LOVE
BEWITCHMENT
MMMM   BEGUILEMENT   BEWILDERMENT
UNSPEAKABLE CRAVING   HORNINESS
THUNDERBOLT   LOVE OF PASTRIES
PENCHANT FOR SMURF DOLLS   BUCKET-O-CLAMS   LUST FOR SHOE HORNS
FREE LOVE   AC/DC   B&D   XYZ
HATE   HUNGRY-MAN DINNER

PUT THEM ALL TOGETHER AND THEY SPELL

LUV.

NEXT: DATING & MATING & HATING & BERATING

LIFE IN
H E DOUBLE L

AN UNPRECEDENTED 13-CHAPTER MINISERIES OF FUN AND MISERY DESIGNED ESPECIALLY FOR YOU.

LOVE IS HELL

CHAPTER III:
THE 9 TYPES OF BOYFRIENDS

LOVESTOMPER'S TEXTBOOK

○ FORBIDDEN CONVERSATION TOPICS IN BED: LOCAL ELECTIONS, SEPTIC TANKS, CHORES, YOUR PARTNER'S SHORTCOMINGS

○

DID ANYONE EVER TELL YOU YOU GRUNT AMUSINGLY WHEN YOU MAKE LOVE?

"JOE SENSITIVE"

AFTER I WASH THE DISHES LET'S CUDDLE, OK?

ALSO KNOWN AS: MR. NICE GUY, FAMILY MAN, HONEY, DARLING, SOFT-BOILED EGG, SNUGGLEPUP.
ADVANTAGES: WELL-BEHAVED; IRONS OWN SHIRTS.
DRAWBACKS: IRRITATINGLY COMPASSIONATE; WIMPY.

"OLD MAN GRUMPUS"

PEOPLE ARE STUPID.

THE WORLD CAN GO TO HELL.

LET'S STAY HOME AND WATCH TV.

ALSO KNOWN AS: GRUMBLES, SOUR PUSS, STICK IN THE MUD, OLD FOGEY, SLOW MOVER, JERK.
ADVANTAGES: STAYS PUT; PREDICTABLE.
DRAWBACKS: ROYAL PAIN IN THE ASS.

"FLINCHY"

I-- I'M SORRY.

FOR WHATEVER IT WAS I DID.

ALSO KNOWN AS: TREMBLY, CREAMPUFF, HEY YOU.
ADVANTAGES: JUMPS ENTERTAININGLY WHEN STARTLED.
DRAWBACKS: EASILY SPOOKED; SURRENDERS WITHOUT A STRUGGLE.

"BIGFOOT"

SHUT YER TRAP, I'M THINKIN'.

ALSO KNOWN AS: CHUNK-STYLE, LUMMOX, IGNORAMUS, GALOOT, THE HULK, BIG 'N' DUMB.
ADVANTAGES: CAN TOTE BALES; IS EASILY FOOLED.
DRAWBACK: CAN BREAK YOU IN HALF; SWEATS LIKE A PIG.

"LAZYBONES"

ZZZZ

ALSO KNOWN AS: LUCKY DOG, PARASITE, BUM, SPONGE, SNOOZE BUCKET, DRUG ADDICT.
ADVANTAGES: WELL RESTED; EASY TARGET.
DRAWBACKS: UNLIKELY TO FULFILL YOUR DREAMS.

"THE SNEAK"

WHO, ME?

ALSO KNOWN AS: LOVE PIRATE, SNAKE, RAT, SLIME, GODDAMNED SON OF A BITCH.
ADVANTAGES: MAY FEEL PANGS OF GUILT.
DRAWBACKS: MAY BE HAVING TIME OF HIS LIFE.

"ACE OF HEARTS"

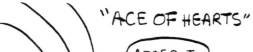

AFTER I WASH THE DISHES LET'S MAKE LOVE LIKE CRAZED WEASELS, OK?

ALSO KNOWN AS: THE SIZZLER, HANDYMAN, DREAMBOAT, CASANOVA, MONSTER.
ADVANTAGES: PERPETUALLY AROUSED.
DRAWBACKS: PERPETUALLY AROUSED.

"THE DREAMER"

SOMEDAY I'M GOING TO BE RICH AND FAMOUS. I DON'T KNOW HOW, BUT--

ALSO KNOWN AS: STRUGGLING ARTIST, PHILOSOPHER, BUFFOON, BAG OF WIND, FOOL.
ADVANTAGES: TELLS GOOD STORIES.
DRAWBACKS: WILL TURN INTO "OLD MAN GRUMPUS"

"MR. RIGHT"

WHILE THE SERVANTS WASH THE DISHES, LET'S MAKE LOVE LIKE CRAZED WEASELS IN MY NEW YACHT, OK?

ALSO KNOWN AS: MR. PERFECT, JIM DANDY, ANSWER TO A WOMAN'S PRAYERS.
DRAWBACKS: HUNTED TO EXTINCTION.

NEXT: THE 9 TYPES OF GIRLFRIENDS.

A 13-CHAPTER CARTOON MINI-SERIES THAT HAS ONLY BEGUN TO FIGHT

(book cover: LOVE IS HELL)

CHAPTER IV: THE 9 TYPES OF GIRLFRIENDS

LOVESTUMPER'S TEXTBOOK

- WHEN GETTING UNDRESSED WITH A NEW FRIEND FOR THE FIRST TIME, DO NOT TRY TO BREAK THE TENSION BY GESTICULATING WILDLY AND MAKING COMICAL THROAT NOISES.

(textbook: GEEBA GEEBA GEEBA)

"MS. NICE GUY"

TICKETS TO THE BOXING MATCH? OH DARLING, YOU SHOULDN'T HAVE.

ALSO KNOWN AS: WHAT A GAL, PRECIOUS, ONE OF THE BOYS, MY MAIN SQUEEZE, DOORMAT.
ADVANTAGES: CHEERFUL, AGREEABLE, KINDLY.
DRAWBACKS: MAY WISE UP SOMEDAY.

"OLD YELLER"

YOU GODDAMNED SPINELESS GOOD-FOR-NOTHING DRAG-ASS NO-TALENT SON OF A BITCH!!! CAN'T YOU SEE YOU'RE MAKING ME MISERABLE??

ALSO KNOWN AS: SHE-DEVIL, SOURPUSS, THE NAG, MY OLD LADY, WARTHOG FROM HELL.
ADVANTAGES: PAYS ATTENTION TO YOU.
DRAWBACKS: SCREECHES, THROWS FRYING PANS.

"SICKLY"

OH, MY HEAD.
MY BACK.
MY CRAMPS.
MY FEET.
MY CELLULITE.

(CHOCOLATE)

ALSO KNOWN AS: WHINER, MEWLER, GLUMPY.
ADVANTAGES: PREDICTABLE.
DRAWBACKS: CONTAGIOUS.

"THE BOSSER"

STAND UP STRAIGHT. PUT ON A DIFFERENT TIE. GET A HAIRCUT. CHANGE YOUR JOB. MAKE SOME MONEY. DON'T GIVE ME THAT LOOK.

ALSO KNOWN AS: WHIPCRACKER, THE SARGE, MS. KNOW-IT-ALL, BALL AND CHAIN, YES MOM.
ADVANTAGES: OFTEN RIGHT.
DRAWBACKS: OFTEN RIGHT, BUT SO WHAT?

"MS. VAGUELY DISSATISFIED"

I JUST CAN'T DECIDE. SHOULD I SWITCH MY CAREER, GOALS, HOME, AND HAIR COLOR?

ALSO KNOWN AS: THE FRETTER, WORRYWART, TYPICAL, AW CMON HONEY.
ADVANTAGES: EASILY SOOTHED.
DRAWBACKS: EVEN MORE EASILY PERTURBED.

"WILD WOMAN OUT OF CONTROL"

I'VE GOT AN IDEA. LEZ GET DRUNK N MAKE LOVE ONNA FRONT LAWN.

I DONE IT BEFORE. S'FUN.

ALSO KNOWN AS: FAST GIRL, FREEWHEELER, GOODTIME CHARLEENA, PASSED OUT.
ADVANTAGES: MORE FUN THAN A BARREL OF MONKEYS.
DRAWBACKS: UNRELIABLE; DRIVES OFF CLIFFS.

"HUFFY"

I SEE NOTHING HUMOROUS IN THOSE SILLY CARTOONS YOU KEEP SNICKERING AT.

(FREUD WAS A JERK)

ALSO KNOWN AS: NO FUN, HUMORLESS PRIG, COLD FISH, CHILLY PROPOSITION, ICEBERG, SNARLY.
ADVANTAGES: YOUR FRIENDS WILL FEEL SORRY FOR YOU.
DRAWBACKS: YOU WILL HAVE NO FRIENDS.

"WOMAN FROM MARS"

I BELIEVE THIS INTERPRETIVE DANCE WILL EXPLAIN HOW I FEEL ABOUT OUR RELATIONSHIP.

ALSO KNOWN AS: THE BABBLER, SPOOKY GIRL, SCREWBALL, LOONY, BAD NEWS, ARTISTIC.
ADVANTAGES: ENTERTAININGLY UNFATHOMABLE.
DRAWBACKS: WILL READ HER POETRY ALOUD.

"MS. DREAMGIRL"

I AM UTTERLY CONTENT WITH YOU JUST THE WAY YOU ARE, MY HANDSOME GENIUS OF A BOYFRIEND.

I THINK WE MUST MAKE LOVE LIKE CRAZED WEASELS NOW.

ALSO KNOWN AS: MS. RIGHT, GODDESS, KNOCK-OUT, PERFECTION, GORGEOUS.
ADVANTAGES: FUNNY, INTELLIGENT, UNINHIBITED.
DRAWBACKS: WILL HAVE NOTHING TO DO WITH YOU.

©1984 BY MATT GROENING

13 BIG CHAPTERS! 7 DONE! 6 TO GO! OVER THE HUMP! SOON TO BE A MAJOR UNPRODUCED SCREENPLAY!

CHAPTER VII: DO YOU **REALLY** WANT TO RISK

LOVEMONKEY'S TEXTBOOK

WHEN IN DOUBT ABOUT HOW TO PROCEED IN LOVE, HEED THE ADVICE OF YOUR CLOSEST FRIENDS.

DON'T LET YER MEATLOAF!!

A SECRET FORBIDDEN ILLICIT TANTALIZING EXOTIC SEXUAL ENCOUNTER WITH A MYSTERIOUS STRANGER?

OR WOULD YOU RATHER JUST READ A CARTOON ABOUT IT?

THE PROS OF LOOSE ANIMALISTIC RUTTING

1. FLEETING MOMENTS OF ECSTASY
2. THE THRILL OF FURTIVENESS.
3. LONELINESS BANISHED FOR AN INSTANT.
4. NEW AND IMPROVED ORGASMS.
5. MIND FREED FROM THINKING ABOUT SEX FOR A FEW MINUTES.

THE MAKING OF THE BEAST WITH TWO BACKS

THIS IS TERRIBLY WRONG — IT'S BAD — OH THE SHAME — IT'S NAUGHTY — FILTHY — DEPRAVED — WE SHOULDN'T BE DOING THIS — CURIOSITY KILLED THE CAT — THE BIBLE FORBIDS THIS — NOT TO MENTION MY DAD — MMM NICE

THE CONS OF FREELY SHARING YOUR LOVE

1. GRUESOME INFECTIONS
2. UNWANTED PREGNANCY
3. BAD REPUTATION
4. PANGS OF GUILT
5. HERPES SIMPLEX
6. HERPES NOT SO SIMPLEX
7. DEPRESSION
8. CHAGRIN
9. SOME WEIRDO DROOLING ON YOU

HINTS FOR HUSSIES

GET DRUNK ENOUGH SO YOU CAN PRETEND YOU DON'T KNOW WHAT YOU'RE DOING

SO YOU WANT TO HAVE A SHAMEFUL AFFAIR

YET SOMEHOW YOU CAN'T JUSTIFY IT

THE NEXT TIME YOU ARE CONTEMPLATING A DECISION IN WHICH YOU ARE DEBATING WHETHER OR NOT TO GO FOR THE GUSTO, ASK YOURSELF THIS IMPORTANT QUESTION: "HOW LONG AM I GOING TO BE DEAD?" WITH THAT PERSPECTIVE, YOU CAN NOW MAKE A FREE, FEARLESS CHOICE TO DO JUST ABOUT ANY GODDAMNED SNEAKY THING YOUR DEVIOUS LITTLE MIND CAN THINK UP. GO AHEAD. HAVE YOUR FUN. YOU'RE WELCOME. GO ON. SEE YOU IN HELL.

TIPS FOR TOADS

DON'T FORGET THE CLITORIS LIKE LAST TIME, DUMMY

DON'T FORGET!

✓ BRING CONTRACEPTIVES
✓ BE HONEST
✓ LEAVE A TRAIL OF BREADCRUMBS SO YOU CAN FIND YOUR WAY HOME

ALWAYS REMEMBER!

✓ S/HE COULD BE A LUNATIC
✓ WHO ARE YOU BETRAYING?
✓ SMILE!!!

20,000,000 B.C. — 1776 — 1945 — YOU ARE HERE — 2001 — 2525 — ETERNITY THIS WAY

LIFESTYLES OF THE RICH AND HELLISH

© 1984 BY MATT GROENING

THE CARTOON THAT BELIEVES THERE'S A POT O' GOLD AT THE BOTTOM O' THE DRAIN

LOVE BE HELL

CHAPTER VIII: SHOULD WE LIVE TOGETHER?

LOVESHOVER'S TEXTBOOK

○ BE CONSIDERATE. AFTER MESMERIZING YOUR FRIENDS FOR HOURS WITH DETAILS OF YOUR LOVE MISERIES, BE SURE TO FEIGN INTEREST WHEN THEY START BABBLING ABOUT THEIR INSIGNIFICANT PROBLEMS.

○

SO I GO, "OH YEAH?" AND SHE GOES "YEAH!!" SO I GO--

FUN • INTIMACY • SECURITY • COMFINESS • SHARING CHORES • WAITING TO USE THE BATHROOM • SNUGGLING • NUZZLING • SAYING "HONEY I'M HOME" • GETTING BACK RUBS • GIVING BACK RUBS • GIVING--YUCK--FOOT RUBS • DID I SAY NUZZLING? • HAVING HALF AS MUCH SPACE IN THE MEDICINE CABINET • CALMLY DISCUSSING BILLS • WATCHING TV • SHOPPING SENSIBLY • FOLDING BLANKETS TOGETHER • SET.

WHETHER YOU CALL IT COHABITATION, HOLY BEDLOCK, PUTTING ON THE DOUBLE HARNESS, GOING DOMESTIC, HAVING IT RIVETED, OR SHACKING UP, LET'S FACE IT-- LIVING TOGETHER CAN BE THE ADVENTURE OF THE DECADE.

DO I HAVE WHAT IT TAKES TO LIVE WITH SOMEONE?

A WEE TEST

Y N
☐ ☐ I HAVE INFINITE PATIENCE WITH MY PARTNER'S CONSTANT BLUNDERS AND STUPIDITIES

☐ ☐ I CAN GET A GOOD NIGHT'S SLEEP EVEN WITH SOMEONE LYING THERE SEETHING NEXT TO ME

☐ ☐ I AM PREPARED TO PLAY SCRABBLE OCCASIONALLY

LIVING TOGETHER SOLVES PROBLEMS!

✓ IF YOU'RE HYPER, LIVING TOGETHER WILL MELLOW YOU OUT.

✓ IF YOU'RE LONELY, LIVING TOGETHER WILL SOOTHE YOUR HEART.

✓ IF YOU'RE AVERAGE, LIVING TOGETHER WILL LAST 2.3 YEARS.

SIGN UP NOW FOR A LIFETIME OF LIVIN' TOGETHER FUN ACTIVITIES

★ MAKING UP NEW RULES

★ GETTING TOGETHER WITH ANOTHER COUPLE FOR DRINKS

★ POKING GENTLE FUN AT YOUR PARTNER'S SLIGHT WEIGHT GAIN

STILL CONFUSED? THEN ASK YOURSELF THIS SLIMY, SELFISH QUESTION:

"WHY BUY THE LOAF WHEN YOU CAN GET FREE SLICES?"

-- OLD BAKED GOODS PROVERB

OF COURSE, LIVING TOGETHER RAISES NEW QUANDARIES

→ WHAT DO YOU MEAN IT'S MY TURN TO DO THE DISHES?

→ I WAS SNORING?

→ IS IT NORMAL TO MAKE LOVE ONCE EVERY THREE MONTHS?

BAT OUT OF HELL

CHAPTER XI: SPLITSVILLE

IT'S MINE — NO, MINE

LOVE IS HELL

LOVESLAMMER'S TEXTBOOK

WHEN HANGING UP ANGRILY ON A LOVER, WATCH THOSE FINGERS!

GO TO HELL!! — SLAM! \\\\ — OW!!!

THE STORY OF A RELATIONSHIP

ONCE UPON A TIME, TWO PEOPLE MET, FELL IN LOVE, AND BEGAN DRIVING EACH OTHER CRAZY.

SOON PETTY BICKERING, BALEFUL STARES, AND DOOR-SLAMMING BECAME THE NORM.

SLAM!!

ONE DAY, ONE OF THE PEOPLE GOT FED UP FOR THE LAST TIME, AND SPLIT FOREVER.

SLAM!!!

LEAVING YOU STRANDED THERE LIKE A BEACHED WHALE.

NOTE: THIS STORY IS ENTIRELY FICTIONAL AND ANY RESEMBLANCE TO INDIVIDUALS LIVING OR DEAD IS PURELY COINCIDENTAL.

HOW TO DUMP YOUR LOVER GENTLY

BE IN A BAD MOOD FOR SEVERAL MONTHS.

CRITICIZE ANYTHING AND EVERYTHING. IF YOU CAN'T SAY SOMETHING MEAN, SAY NOTHING AT ALL.

HONE YOUR JOYLESSNESS.

STOP HAVING SEX.

EAT MEALS IN SILENCE.

WHEN QUESTIONED, REFUSE TO SAY WHAT YOU ARE THINKING.

WHEN THE PROPER MOMENT COMES, LOWER THE BOOM.

THEN SCRAM.

DIVIDING UP THE GOODIES

THAT ZENITH HOME ENTERTAINMENT CENTER IS MINE.

BUT I NEED IT.

THE EXIT RETORT

SLAM!!

YOU'LL BE BACK!!

THE DESPERATE PLEA

PLEASE! DON'T LEAVE ME! I'LL DO ANYTHING!!

GET THE **HELL** OUT OF MY WAY.

DON'T GO YET! I'LL DO MY LITTLE CHARLESTON DANCE!! YOU **LOVE** THAT!

THE WAIT

IF YOU ARE DUMPED

REMEMBER, LIFE WAS ONCE BEAUTIFUL AND FOOD DIDN'T TASTE LIKE CARDBOARD.

PUNCH YOUR PILLOW, NOT THE WALL.

DON'T ACT ON ANY BRIGHT IDEAS YOU SUDDENLY GET, SUCH AS SHAVING YOUR HEAD OR PICKING FIGHTS WITH BURLY THUGS.

DO NOT LOATHE YOURSELF. YOU ARE NO MORE AN UNLOVABLE PATHETIC JERK THAN YOU EVER WERE.

THERE IS MORE THAN ONE CUTTLEFISH IN THE SEA.

DUMPISM DO'S AND DON'TS

WOULD IT BE OK IF I SLEPT OUTSIDE YOUR DOOR TONIGHT? I WON'T MAKE ANY NOISE.

DON'T HUMILIATE YOURSELF.

DO LEARN WHEN TO GIVE UP.

I THOUGHT YOU SAID YOU BROKE UP WITH BINKY.

I BRAKE FOR NO ONE!!

DON'T TAKE YOUR PAIN OUT ON THE REST OF THE WORLD.

DO STEW IN YOUR OWN JUICES.

LOVE. HA. THAT'S A LAUGH.

1001 FACES OF YOUR LOVER

WIFE IN HELL

©1983 BY MATT GROENING

THE FOOL

MR. PERFECT

THE WORM

JOE SENSITIVE

BIGFOOT

SEX MACHINE

THE CUDDLER

THE TWO-FACED LIAR

MY DARLING

6 SIMPLE TECHNIQUES TO KEEP YOUR MAIN LOVE RELATIONSHIP ALIVE & KICKING

A PEACEFUL LONG-TERM LOVE-TYPE RELATIONSHIP CAN OFTEN BE LIKENED TO A SLOW BOAT TO CHINA, PUTTERING ALONG THROUGH THE MURKY WATERS NIGHT AFTER NIGHT, MONTH AFTER MONTH, YEAR AFTER YEAR, WHILE YOU AND YOUR LOVE MATEY JUST SIT THERE IN THE BOILER ROOM STOKIN' THE FIRE, CHECKIN' THE PRESSURE GAUGE, OR WATCHIN' CABLE TV. SOUNDS PRETTY BORING, DOESN'T IT? WELL, DON'T DESPAIR-- BY CAREFULLY USING THIS SCIENTIFIC GUIDE, YOU CAN TURN YOUR OWN TEDIOUS LOVE-STEAMSHIP INTO AN ASSERTIVE NUCLEAR-POWERED SUBMARINE OF LUST, EXCITEMENT, AND YELLING.

① PULL A SWITCHEROO.
CONSTANT AFFECTION GETS STALE AFTER A WHILE, SO THE NEXT TIME YOU TALK TO YOUR PARTNER, MIX THE SIGNALS.

I LOVE YOU, LARD-ASS.

② SHOW CONCERN FOR YOUR LOVER'S SHORTCOMINGS.
THIS TECHNIQUE IS ACTUALLY QUITE GRATIFYING. ALL YOU HAVE TO DO IS SUBTLY POINT OUT YOUR PARTNER'S DEFECTS AND BLUNDERS. AVOID BEING CRUEL WHEN POSSIBLE BY PHRASING YOUR REMARKS IN THE FORM OF PROBING QUESTIONS.

HOW CAN YOU BE SO STUPID?

③ RESIST THE IMPULSE TO APOLOGIZE.
YOUR PARTNER WILL JUST REALIZE YOU'RE GETTING WEARY, SO YOU'VE GOT TO MAINTAIN YOUR UNYIELDING INTEGRITY. EITHER THAT OR WORD YOUR APOLOGY SO THAT YOU DON'T LOSE FACE.

YOU BETTER WATCH IT.

I'M SORRY YOU GOT ANGRY WHEN I CALLED YOU A STUPID LARD-ASS.

④ RECOGNIZE THAT YOUR MATE'S UNHAPPINESS IS NOT YOUR RESPONSIBILITY.
IT'S A DOG-EAT-DOG WORLD OUT THERE, SO WHY SHOULD IT BE ANY DIFFERENT AT HOME? LISTEN PATIENTLY TO YOUR PARTNER'S PROBLEMS, THEN REPLY WITH AN OBJECTIVE SUMMARY.

YOU KNOW WHAT YOUR PROBLEM IS? YOUR PROBLEM IS YOU'RE PATHETIC.

⑤ REPEAT THE THREE MAGIC WORDS.
SOMETIMES YOU'RE JUST NOT IN THE MOOD FOR A COMPLICATED DISCUSSION WITH YOUR PARTNER. WHEN THIS IS THE CASE, USE THE FOLLOWING THREE MAGIC WORDS TO GET YOUR WAY. YOU MAY HAVE TO REPEAT THE WORDS SEVERAL TIMES, BUT EVENTUALLY THEY **WILL** WORK.

OH SHUT UP.

⑥ TEMPER YOUR HOSTILITY WITH CLEVERNESS AND HUMOR.
YOU CAN TRANSFORM YOUR NASTIEST FEELINGS INTO MOMENTS OF LEVITY BY COMMUNICATING THEM IN THE FORM OF SUBTLE, WITTY JOKES.

I DON'T LOVE YOU ANYMORE. JUST KIDDING.

THE RELATIONSHIP
A BALLET

WHAT NOT TO SAY DURING MOMENTS OF INTIMACY

©1982 BY MATT GROENING ASSISTED BY WINDY TAMKIN

HELL / E life in L / L L E / LLEH

9 SECRET LOVE TECHNIQUES
THAT COULD POSSIBLY TURN MEN INTO PUTTY IN YOUR HANDS

© 1982 BY M. GROENING

WOMEN: MEN! WHAT A WORLD, HUH? IN THE OLD DAYS EVERYTHING WAS EASY, WITH TRUE LOVE AND HEARTS AND FLOWERS AND FRILLY DRESSES AND LIGHT PETTING AND SING-ALONG HAYRIDES -- BUT NOWADAYS EVERYTHING IS SCREWY. YOU ALWAYS GOTTA BE ON GUARD, BECAUSE NO ONE CAN BE TRUSTED -- NOT EVEN YOUR FAVORITE LOVER. IT'S SAD IN A WAY. BUT WE CAN'T JUST GIVE UP. A MAN WITHOUT A WOMAN IS LIKE A TUGBOAT IN A LOGJAM. A WOMAN WITHOUT A MAN IS LIKE A FISH RUN OVER BY A BICYCLE. HENCE THIS HERE GUIDE, TO HELP WOMEN HELP MEN TO SEE THE LOVE LIGHT.

① DAZZLE 'EM. FACE IT. MEN ARE DOPES -- GORILLAS -- SWEATY, LUMBERING BEASTS -- AND TO GET THEIR ATTENTION YOU HAVE TO FOOL 'EM -- TRICK 'EM -- PRACTICALLY WHACK 'EM ON THE NOSE WITH A ROLLED UP NEWSPAPER.

> HEY -- WHAT FOR YOU WHACK ME ONNA NOSE WITH A ROLLED UP NEWSPAPER?
> SAY -- WHAT IS THAT INTRIGUINGLY PROVOCATIVE PERFUME YOU'RE WEARING?

② FEIGN INTEREST IN THEIR TEDIOUS JABBER. MEN DIG IT WHEN THEY CAN BABBLE ON ENDLESSLY YEAR AFTER YEAR ABOUT GUNS, BLIMPS, AND CIGARS WITHOUT BEING CHALLENGED TO CHANGE THE SUBJECT. ALL YOU HAVE TO DO IS LEARN A FEW SIMPLE WORDS AND DEVELOP A CAPACITY FOR LENGTHY MONOLOGUES ON CARBURETORS, HOME COMPUTERS, AND CURLY OF THE THREE STOOGES.

> RILLY?
> MY GOODNESS.
> RILLY?

③ ACT PETULANT. FOR SOME WEIRD REASON, MEN GET A CHARGE OUT OF SEEING WOMEN GETTING REALLY STEAMED -- PARTICULARLY WHEN IT'S ABOUT SOMETHING TRIVIAL, LIKE A RUN IN YOUR STOCKING OR EQUAL PAY FOR EQUAL WORK. JUST STOMP YOUR FOOT ON THE FLOOR, STICK OUT YOUR LOWER LIP, UTTER A LIGHT OBSCENITY, AND LISTEN FOR THAT CONDESCENDING, INDULGENT MALE CHUCKLE THAT SAYS, "WHATSAMATTA, BABY?"

> MY YOU LOOK PRETTY WHEN YOU'RE PSYCHOPATHIC.

④ BE UNFATHOMABLE. ONE THING THAT KEEPS MEN HOOKED IS WHEN THEY CAN'T FIGURE OUT WHAT THE HELL IS GOING ON. THIS IS EASY -- JUST THINK OF YOURSELF AS A FAUCET THAT RUNS BOILING HOT OR ICY COLD WITHOUT WARNING. MEN WON'T LIKE IT, BUT THEY HAVE BEEN KNOWN TO SPEND ENTIRE LIFETIMES TRYING TO UNDERSTAND IT.

> I LOVE YOU.
> I LOVE YOU TOO.
> YOU DON'T KNOW WHAT LOVE IS.
> HUH?
> PLEASE -- LET'S NOT FIGHT. I LOVE YOU.

⑤ SLIP INTO SOMETHING A BIT MORE COMFORTABLE. GET ALL DOLLED UP AND COME ON LIKE GANGBUSTERS. NOTHING CAN SWAY A WOULD-BE DREAMBOAT LIKE RUBY RED LIPS, THREE-INCH PAINTED FINGERNAILS, A PEEK-A-BOO BLOUSE, AND SEE-THRU PANTIES. WORKS LIKE A VOODOO CHARM.

> YIKES.

⑥ ACCEDE TO THEIR SICKO EROTIC REQUESTS. MEN CAN BE LIKENED TO RUTTING GRIZZLY BEARS, SNURFLING WOLVERINES, OR SEX-CRAZED WHITE RABBITS WITH JUST ONE THING ON THEIR DISGUSTING MINDS. ACTUALLY, YOU CAN PLAY IT TWO WAYS: EITHER FUCK THEIR BRAINS OUT, FOR WHICH YOU WILL BE REWARDED WITH DOGLIKE DEVOTION, OR WITHHOLD ALL SEXUAL FAVORS TILL LATER, FOR WHICH YOU WILL BE REWARDED WITH DOGLIKE DEVOTION.

> OOH BABY I LOVE IT WHEN WE CUDDLE.
> MMM HMM.
> LISTEN MISTER KEEP YER GRUBBY PAWS TO YERSELF.

⑦ MAKE 'EM WHISTLE A DIFFERENT TUNE. MEN ARE BASICALLY QUIVERING, SPINELESS JELLYFISH JUST FLOATING ALONG IN LIFE -- BUT WITH THE RIGHT AMOUNT OF PUSHING, PRODDING, AND NAGGING, YOU CAN IMPROVE THEM -- FROM HOPELESSLY INSENSITIVE OAFS INTO HOPELESSLY SENSITIVE OAFS. REMEMBER: KEEP AT IT.

> STRAIGHTEN UP, HONEY -- YOU'RE SLOUCHING.
> TAKE THAT TOOTHPICK OUT OF YOUR MOUTH. IT'S VULGAR.
> YOU'LL THANK ME FOR THIS SOMEDAY.
> DON'T GIVE ME THAT LOOK. IT'S UNBECOMING.

⑧ DEFLATE 'EM. IT'S SURPRISINGLY EASY TO PUNCTURE THE EGOS OF SLOW-WITTED MALE BEHEMOTHS WITH A QUICK VERBAL JAB OR AN UNYIELDING MORAL/POLITICAL EXHORTATION. CURIOUSLY, MEN FEEL A TREMENDOUS AMOUNT OF GUILT THAT IS HELD IN CHECK ONLY BY AN EQUALLY HEFTY LOAD OF UNFOCUSED RAGE -- AND YOU CAN WORK THIS TO YOUR ADVANTAGE.

> HEY LOOK AT THIS SILLY CARTOON.
> WHY, IN THIS TIME OF CHANGING VALUES AND FEMALE LIBERATION, DO MEN PERSIST IN LAUGHING AT WOMEN?
> I -- I AM FILLED WITH SHAME.

⑨ PUT YOUR ARM AROUND YOUR HONEY, READ THIS CARTOON ALOUD TOGETHER, AND SAY: "AREN'T YOU GLAD WE'RE BEYOND ALL THIS?"

LIFE IN HE

CALLING ALL MEN! — CALLING ALL MEN!

©1982 BY MATT GROENING

9 SECRET LOVE TECHNIQUES WOMEN FIND WELL-NIGH IRRESISTIBLE

FOR MEN ONLY

NO BATTERIES

AS SEEN ON TV

VOID WHERE PROHIBITED

MEN! EVER MEET THAT SPECIAL FEMALE LADY PERSON OF OUR FAIR SEX, THE WOMEN, AND SHE GIVE YOU A LOOK LIKE YOU WAS A WARTHOG FROM HELL? LOTS OF TIMES? WELL LISTEN, BRO, THINGS COULD BE PLENTY DIFFERENT ONCE YOU MASTER THE **9 SECRET LOVE TECHNIQUES WOMEN FIND WELL-NIGH IRRESPONSIBLE.** PLENTY DIFFERENT.

SO SETTLE DOWN, TAKE OFF THEM BOOTS, CHOW DOWN ON A HUNGRY-MAN TV DINNER AND A BOTTLE OF LITE BEER, BELCH A COUPLE TIMES, RUB YER FACE, LET OUT A WHOOP, SPIT ON THE FLOOR, AND CHECK THIS OUT.

③. BE MASCULINE!

*MASCULINE = LIKE A MAN

THAT'S RIGHT! MOVE YER ARMS AROUND. FLEX YER MUSCLES. PUFF OUT YER CHEST. STAND UP STRAIGHT. SWAGGER DOWN THE STREET. SQUINT. SNARL. SNEER. MUTTER ANGRY GIBBERISH TO NO ONE IN PARTICULAR. DON'T TAKE NO GUFF.

GRUNT / GRRR / FEH

⑥. LISTEN AT HER! UH HUH! NOTHING--

BUT NOTHING--PUTS A WOMAN OFFGUARD LIKE IF SHE THINKS YER PAYING ATTENTION TO HER CEASELESS PRATTLE. MEANWHILES, YOU GOT SOME IMPORTANT THINKING OF YER OWN TO GET DONE -- SO YOU GOTTA LEARN THE SUBTLE GESTURES AND MURMURS THAT'LL KEEP YOU OUT OF HOT WATER! HOO DOGGIES!

MY MY. / HMMM. / IS THAT SO? / WELL AIN'T THAT A CORKER.

①. CLEAN UP YER ACT! THAT'S RIGHT! TAKE A SHOWER EVERY WEEK AND SCRUB THAT GRIT OFF! THE SMELLY CAVEMAN LOOK SO POPULAR LAST SEASON IS DEFINITELY DÉCLASSÉ NOWADAYS.

WHERZA GURLS? / DON'T BE A DIP-- TAKE A DIP / YUK / YUM

④. COPY HER GESTURES! YEP! DRIVES 'EM WILD. IF SHE LEANS FORWARD, YOU LEAN FORWARD. IF SHE SCRATCHES HER NOSE, YOU SCRATCH YOUR OWN [#IMPORTANT] NOSE. THIS SHOWS YOU ARE BOTH SYNCHRONIZED WITH THE UNIVERSE OR SOMETHING. WORKS LIKE A CHARM.

ARE YOU MOCKING ME? / NO. / HELP! POLICE!

⑦. GIVE HER THE OLD ONCE-OVER! NYUP! WHEN A GUY LOOKS A WOMAN UP AND DOWN, FROM THE TOP OF HER NEW PERM TO THE BOTTOM OF HER STILETTO HEELS, IT'S LIKE SAYING, "YOU'RE THE HOSTESS WITH THE MOSTEST!" THIS COURTSHIP RITUAL IS USED THE WORLD OVER, FROM THE LOWLIEST SEA SLUG TO OUR MOST EMINENT BRAINY SCIENCE GUYS.

GOL! SHUCKS! WOO WOO! OOH LA LA! MERCI BEAUCOUPS! I YI YI!

②. GET A NICKNAME! THAT'S RIGHT! NOTHING PIQUES THE CURIOSITY OF A WOMAN LIKE AN EVOCATIVE NICKNAME. TATOO IT ON YOUR CHEST FOR EASY REFERENCE.

EXAMPLES
"POWERHOUSE"
"MAD DOG"
"ELVIS"
"BIG PEE WEE"
"JANITOR IN A DRUM"

--BUT MY FRIENDS CALL ME "CHUNK-STYLE." / BINKY

⑤. PREEN YERSELF BUT GOOD! THAT'S NO JIVE! WOMEN DIG THAT EXTRA TOUCH THAT TELLS 'EM "THIS GUY IS NIFTY." THINGS LIKE A SPORTY NEW HAIRCUT, BLINKING CHEST MEDALLION, OR HANDY PENCIL TUCKED BEHIND THE EAR. REMEMBER: YOU CAN NEVER USE TOO MUCH AFTERSHAVE LOTION.

HEY. WANNA SEE MY WRIST-CALCULATOR? / BIP BIP

⑧. SHOW HER WHO'S BOSS! WATCH OUT! THIS ONE'S A DOOZY, WHAT WITH ALL THE DING-DANG FUSS OVER "EQUALITY," "FREEDOM," AND "JUSTICE." BUT IF YOU STICK TO YER GUNS, JUT OUT YER CHIN LIKE A TOUGH GUY, AND BELLOW "AHH, SHUDDUP" ENOUGH TIMES, SHE'LL GET THE MESSAGE. REMEMBER: SOME WOMEN ARE EASIER TO FOOL THAN OTHERS.

I SAID GETCHER ASS IN HERE. / WHAT? / OH-- NOTHING.

⑨. GIVE HER THIS GUIDE, DROP TO YER KNEES, YELP LIKE A WOUNDED PUP, AND SAY: "I GUESS I'M JUST TOO SENSITIVE."

HOW BE MANLY IN THIS TROUBLE TIMES

ALL RIGHT CAN THE CHATTER YOU MONKEYS AND LISTEN UP. SCUSE US LADIES WE GOT MEN TALK HERE. WHILE YER UP YOU MIND GETTING US SOME COFFEE? OK MEN. WHAT THE HELL IS HAPPENING TO US? WHERE DID WE GO WRONG? ONE MINUTE WE'RE SWINGING THROUGH TREES SNAGGLING FRESH TROUTS WITH OUR BARE HANDS BEATING UP WEAKER MEMBERS OF THE TRIBE. NEXT MINUTE WE'RE CRAWLING AROUND ON THE FLOOR LOOKING FOR CONTACT LENSES WEARING PERFUME READING GQ HONKING HORN IN TRAFFIC JAMS LIKE TINY SQUEAKER MICE. SO COME ON MEN! BUTTS IN GEAR! GRUFFY! FORWARD HUP! MOVE EM OUT! GET IT UP!

YABBADABBADOO!

DIG WE MUST
MEN AT WORK + PLAY

BOWL FOR TROPHIES
FLEX MUSCLES
WAX HOTROD
SHAVE FACE
SHOOT INTRUDERS
EJACULATE

WE GOT PROBLEMS
LITTLE PROBLEMS + BIG PROBLEMS

DRAB ATTIRE
STUMPY FINGERNAILS
NICK FACE SHAVE
GOLFBALL IN LAKE
FALL OUT OF HAMMOCK
EJACULATE TOO SPEEDY
NUMB

ASPERSIONS AGAINST MENS DIGNITY AND PROWESS

"BEAU" "BUSTER" "BUB" "DIP"
"BIG FELLA" "LITTLE CHUM" "BOY"
"GORILLA" "BEAST" "APE" "HONEY"
"JERK" AND SEVERAL MORE.

EEK MY LEATHER PANTS ARE CHAFING.

MODERN MAN

MEN OPPRESSED BY CRUEL LANGUAGE TRICKS

MANIAC   MANSLAUGHTER MANGLE
PORTUGUESE MAN O' WAR MANNEQUIN
MENSTRUATION MENTALLY UNBALANCED
MANILLA ENVELOPES HEEBIE JEEBIES

MAN TO MAN ADVICE:

"TO BE MANLY YOU MUST DO MANLY."

YELL AT CARS. HUFF AND PUFF. YELL AT TV. HUNT CRITTERS. YELL AT WIFE. STOMP OUT OF HOUSE. YELL AT GOD. SHOP AT LIQUOR STORE. YELL AT WOMEN ON STREET. PUNCH STRANGERS.

THE PROBLEM WITH WOMEN

OH MAN. WHOOPS. SHHH-- HERE THEY COME.

SO HOW I BE MANLY WHEN I FEEL LIKE CONFUSE SQUEAK TOY?

SHAPE UP OR SHIP OUT, POPS.

THE MANLY MAN KNOW WHAT HE WANT.

I NEED SOME ARTIFICIAL SWEETENER FOR MY COFFEE, DAMN IT.

HMPH. I'LL GET IT MYSELF.

FILE UNDER HELL

OK, SO THERE WAS THIS LADY AND SHE HAD THIS LITTLE PET DOG. AND FOR SOME REASON THE LITTLE DOG'S NAME WAS FREESHOW. OK? SO ONE DAY THE LADY TOOK OFF ALL HER CLOTHES AND SHE WENT INTO THE BATHTUB. SO THE LITTLE DOG SUDDENLY JUMPS OUT THE WINDOW WHEN SHE ISN'T LOOKING, RIGHT? AND SO THE LADY SEES HE'S GONE, AND SHE JUST JUMPS OUT OF THE BATHTUB AND GOES RUNNING DOWN THE STREET, AND SHE'S YELLING "FREESHOW! FREESHOW!"

©1985 BY MATT GROENING

KIDS' QUESTIONS ABOUT DEATH

WHEN YOU GO TO HEAVEN, DO YOU LOOK LIKE HOW YOU DID WHEN YOU DIED?

IF YOUR LEG GETS AMPUTATED DURING YOUR LIFE, IS IT WAITING FOR YOU IN HEAVEN?

CAN DEAD PEOPLE IN COFFINS HEAR WHAT YOU'RE SAYING?

WELL, HE LIVED A FULL AND REWARDING LIFE, SORT OF.

SURE LOOKS PEACEFUL, DON'T HE?

PLEASE-- SHUT UP-- I BEG OF YOU

IF CATS ARE BAD, DO THEY GO TO CAT HELL?

MEOW

MEOW

MEWL

MEOW

MEOW

ARE THERE CAVEMEN IN HEAVEN?

IF I GO TO HEAVEN, WILL I HAVE ANY FRIENDS?

WON'T ETERNITY GET KIND OF BORING AFTER AWHILE?

WILL I GO TO HELL JUST FOR ASKING THESE QUESTIONS?

LIFE IN HELL

© 1984 BY MATT GROENING

YOUR GUIDE TO THE MODERN CREATIVE ARTISTIC TYPES

CREATIVE ARTISTIC TYPE	DOMINANT PERSONALITY TRAIT	SECONDARY PERSONALITY TRAITS	DISTINGUISHING FEATURES	HAUNTING QUESTION	HOW TO ANNOY THEM
WRITER	SELF-ABSORPTION	POMPOSITY IRRITABILITY WHINING	NERVOUS TWITCHING, BAD POSTURE	"AM I JUST A HACK?"	SAY: BUT HOW DO YOU MAKE A LIVING?
PAINTER	SELF-OBSESSION	DELUSIONS OF GRANDEUR	SPATTERED PANTS, INARTICULATE EXPLANATIONS	"SHOULD I MOVE TO NEW YORK?"	SAY: IT'S NOT FINISHED, IS IT?
POET	SELF-PITY	PARANOIA BITTERNESS BILE	WEIRD LIPS SNIVELING POVERTY	"WHY DOES EVERYONE AVOID ME?"	BE ANOTHER POET.
PERFORMANCE ARTIST	SELF-INDULGENCE	ALIENATION IRRATIONALITY SHAMELESSNESS	VAGUELY PUNKISH LOOK, ONLY WITH WRINKLED SKIN	"GIVEN THE INFINITE NUMBER OF THINGS I COULD DO WITH MY LIFE, WHY AM I STANDING HERE ONSTAGE SLAPPING MEAT ON MY HEAD?"	SAY: I SAW SOMETHING JUST LIKE THAT ONCE ON THE GONG SHOW.
ACTOR	SELF-DEVOTION	SELF-DOUBT	AURA OF INSINCERITY	"DO I HAVE ANY TALENT?"	SAY: PUT ON A FEW POUNDS, HAVEN'T YOU?
ROCK & ROLL GUITARIST	SELF-COMPLACENCY	SLEAZINESS SLIMINESS SMUGNESS	SALLOW COMPLEXION, VENEREAL SCABS	"WHERE AM I?"	THROW BEER BOTTLES AT THEIR HEADS DURING CONCERTS.
STREET MIME	SELF-SATISFACTION	COMPULSION TO PESTER	SCRAWNY BOD TORN LEOTARDS IMPISH BEHAVIOR	"HAVE I NO SHAME?"	PUNCH 'EM IN THE MOUTH.
CARTOONIST	MALICIOUS FRIVOLITY	FRIVOLOUS MALICIOUSNESS	INKY FINGERS INKY SHIRTS INKY PANTS	"WILL I BE DRAWING GODDAMNED RABBITS FOR THE REST OF MY LIFE?"	IT IS UNWISE TO ANNOY CARTOONISTS.

HOW TO BE A CLEVER FILM CRITIC

ARE YOU QUALIFIED TO BE A CLEVER FILM CRITIC?

☐ DID YOU HAVE NO FRIENDS AS A CHILD?

☐ DO YOU SALIVATE AT THE SMELL OF STALE POPCORN?

☐ DO YOU THRILL AT THE PROSPECT OF SPENDING A CAREER WRITING IN-DEPTH ANALYSES OF MOVIES AIMED AT SUBLITERATE 15-YEAR-OLDS?

☐ DO YOU MIND BEING LOATHED FOR YOUR CLEVER OPINIONS?

HOW TO PAD OUT A CLEVER FILM REVIEW WHEN YOU DON'T HAVE ANYTHING TO SAY

☐ RECOUNT THE PLOT

☐ THROW IN GRATUITOUS PUNS

☐ WRITE ABOUT YOURSELF

FOR ADVANCED CLEVER FILM CRITICS ONLY!

CAN YOU USE "MISE-EN-SCÈNE" IN A REVIEW THAT ANYONE WILL FINISH READING?

BLOODSHOT EYES

BAGS

FRAYED COLLAR

ACHING BACK

ACHING BUTT

ACHING HEAD

PALLID COMPLEXION

NERVOUS TWITCH DUE TO DEADLINE PRESSURE

THESAURUS

DEVELOP A CLEVER RATING SYSTEM THAT REDUCES YOUR CRITIQUES TO CUTE 'N' EASY CONSUMER GUIDES

☆☆☆ STARS ARE FUN!

9½ NUMBERS ARE IN!

☺☺☺ HOW ABOUT SMILEYS?

$$$$ OR DOLLAR SIGNS??

DON'T FORGET CINEMA'S GREATEST PARADOX

? ? ? ? ? ? ? ? ? ?

THE FRENCH ARE FUNNY.

SEX IS FUNNY.

AND COMEDIES ARE FUNNY.

YET NO FRENCH SEX COMEDIES ARE FUNNY.

THE 4 TYPES OF CLEVER FILM CRITICS

WHICH DO YOU ASPIRE TO BE?

ACADEMIC TYPE	SERIOUS TYPE	DAILY TYPE	TV CLOWN
BORING, UNREADABLE	REVEALS ENDINGS	NICE PLOT SUMMARIES	NICE SWEATERS

CLEVER WORDS TO USE IN REVIEWS SO AS TO ENSURE YOU WILL BE QUOTED IN FILM ADS

PICK ONE FROM COLUMN A AND ONE FROM COLUMN B

COLUMN A	COLUMN B
ADVERBS	ADJECTIVES
RICHLY	HAUNTING
MARVELOUSLY	TOUCHING
WONDERFULLY	ABSORBING
ODDLY	EVOCATIVE
PROVOCATIVELY	COMPELLING
REFRESHINGLY	ELEGANT
STUNNINGLY	ORIGINAL

AND DON'T FORGET THESE HANDY PHRASES:

"I LOVED IT!"

"IT SIZZLES!"

"...GREAT FUN..."

"A MASTERPIECE!"

IF YOU CAN'T BE A CLEVER FILM CRITIC, MAYBE YOU CAN BE:

☐ A SNIVELING CINEMA ENTHUSIAST WHO ACTUALLY TRIES TO TALK LIKE A CLEVER FILM CRITIC IN CASUAL CONVERSATION

☐ A FILM BUFF SO DEVOTED TO THE MEDIUM THAT YOU HAVE OPINIONS OF MOVIES YOU HAVEN'T SEEN

☐ ONE OF THOSE SQUEAKERS WHO WRITES IRATE LETTERS TO CLEVER FILM CRITICS

HOW TO BE A SENSITIVE POET

HOW TO TELL IF YOU ARE THE SENSITIVE-POET TYPE

YES NO
- ☐ ☐ ARE YOU "DIFFERENT"?
- ☐ ☐ DO YOU FEEL "SPECIAL"?
- ☐ ☐ ARE YOU "COMPLICATED"?
- ☐ ☐ DO YOU ENJOY "POVERTY"?

YOUR ANSWERS REALLY DON'T MATTER. JUST REMEMBER:
- ★ IN A COSMIC SENSE, EVERYONE IS A SENSITIVE POET.
- ★ RECOGNITION ISN'T EVERYTHING.
- ★ NOTHING IS IMPOSSIBLE.

BEGINNING EXERCISES FOR SENSITIVE POETS

YOU WILL NEED:
PENCIL   PAPER   SOMBER CLOTHING

PRINTED BELOW ARE FIRST LINES OF SENSITIVE POEMS. READ THEM. LET YOUR MIND DRIFT. SET YOUR SOULFULNESS FREE. GO INTO A TRANCE. NOW FINISH THE POEMS.

I SAW A GENIUS IN THE MIRROR TODAY....

ACROSS THE LONELY BEACH I WANDER....

NEAR THE LONELY KNOLL I WEEP....

ON THE LONELY CLIFF I LOITER....

ALAS, THE HORNETS BUZZING IN MY BRAIN....

(BE SURE TO CREDIT THIS CARTOON WHEN YOUR POEMS GET PUBLISHED.)

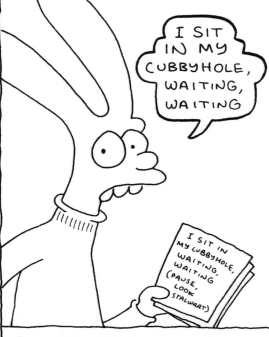

I SIT IN MY CUBBYHOLE, WAITING, WAITING

I SIT IN MY CUBBYHOLE, WAITING, WAITING, (PAUSE, LOOK STALWART)

SUBJECTS FOR SENSITIVE POEMS

AUTUMN   DEATH PAIN TREES
THE COSMOS CRITICS   BEAUTY
CLOUDS SUICIDE DREAMING
LEAVES YOURSELF LONELINESS
FUTILITY BLIGHT DEPRESSION
DECAY LOSS ENTROPY LOVE
FLOWERS BRANCHES TREE STUMPS

DO YOU HAVE THE GUTS TO BE A SENSITIVE POET?

NAY O YES
- ☐ ☐ CAN YOU FACE DISDAIN?
- ☐ ☐ CAN YOU FACE RIDICULE?
- ☐ ☐ CAN YOU FACE UTTER INDIFFERENCE?

ADVANCED EXERCISES FOR SENSITIVE POETS

YOU WILL NEED:
PENCIL   PAPER   BITTERNESS

1. WRITE A POEM FROM THE POINT OF VIEW OF A CREAKY OLD BARN (HINT: " I AM A BARN, CREAKING, CREAKING")

2. WRITE A SONNET ABOUT YOUR MOM.

3. WRITE A POEM ABOUT A FLEETING EMOTION UNIQUE TO YOU, USING A COMPLEX AND PRIVATE SYSTEM OF SYMBOLS THAT NO ONE ELSE CAN POSSIBLY UNDERSTAND.

HOW TO BE A PROFESSIONAL SENSITIVE POET

MISTY VAPORS A POETRY QUARTERLY

SUBMIT YOUR POEMS TO PUBLICATIONS YOU DON'T READ

FISHIN' ILLUSTRATED

SUBMIT YOUR POEMS TO PUBLICATIONS THAT DON'T PRINT POETRY

CULTIVATE A SNEERING HATRED OF ALL OTHER SENSITIVE POETS

AND REMEMBER: WHEN IN ELKVILLE, BE SURE TO STOP BY THE TOMB OF THE UNKNOWN SENSITIVE POET AND SET A SPELL.

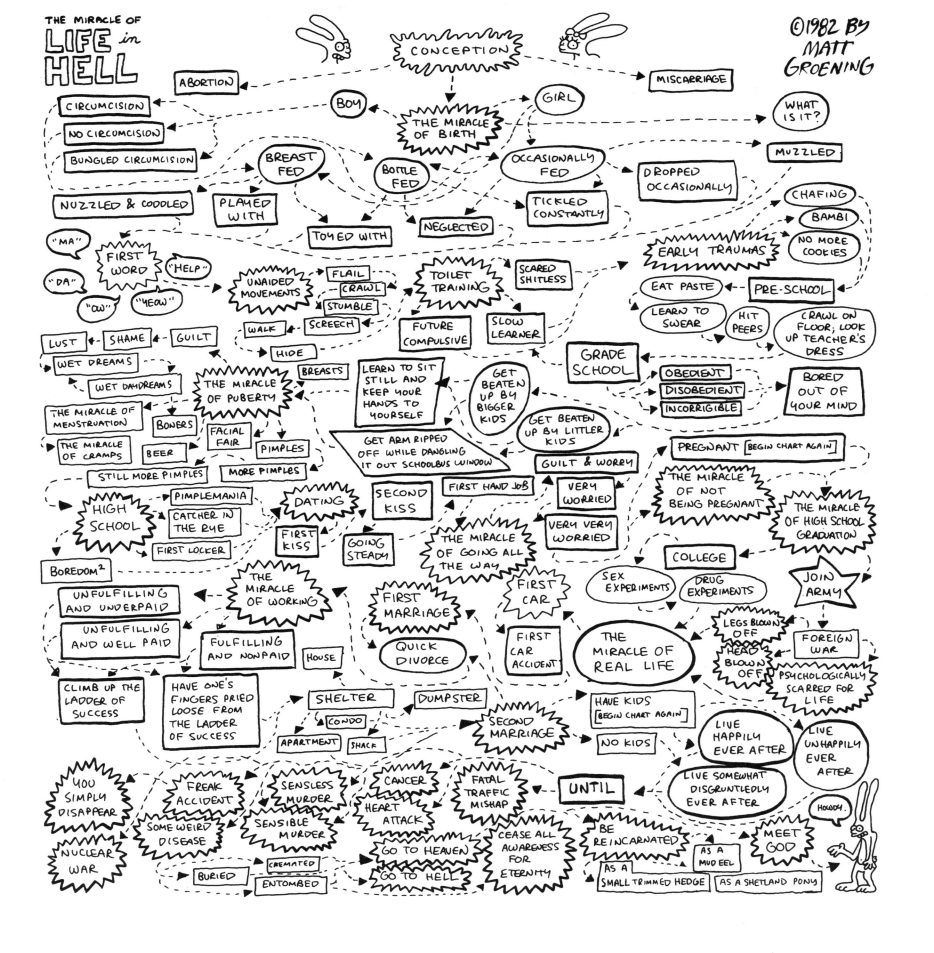

About the Author

Matt Groening's weekly comic strip "Life in Hell"® appears in more than 250 newspapers around the world, and has been collected in eleven books, most of which have the word "Hell" in the title. Groening is also the creator of the animated TV series *The Simpsons*, and founder of Bongo Comics Group, which began publishing in 1993. He lives in Los Angeles.

FLASH!

Continue your tour of this hellish life with these other books by Matt Groening, all available from Pantheon.